26.6.

F

FRIENDSHIP

by
Georgette Butcher

in the series
Quiet Times

Collins

FOUNT PAPERBACKS

William Collins Sons & Co. Ltd
London • Glasgow • Sydney • Auckland •
Toronto • Johannesburg

First published in Great Britain in 1990 by Fount
Paperbacks

Fount Paperbacks is an imprint of
Collins Religious Division,
part of the Collins Publishing Group
8 Grafton Street, London W1X 3LA

Printed in England by Clays Ltd, St Ives plc

Friendship

Yes, the One who watches over you is your friend.

I Am With You

The emphasis by the word "yes" reminds that God is indeed our friend but also that his is a perfect friendship, so that whilst we may rejoice in wonderful friendships, God's love is even greater. His concern for us is entire; nothing about us can shock him; he wants nothing but the best for each one of us. He does not condemn us for our weaknesses; longs only that we should bring him into all our desires, joys, sorrows, pain, decisions.

He wants us to know and remember that he is our friend. He is not someone on whom we call occasionally, as we might do with an earthly friend, but one who wants to be a part of everything that we are and do. It means that he is for us, and that we are protected by his care. A true friend will tell us the truth about ourselves, and this too is a part of God's love and friendship. His purpose is to make us like himself, so he will teach us the lessons that we need to learn in order to bring us closer to this desire; but always, he is our friend.

The wounds incurred in spiritual battle come, unfortunately,
all too often from friendly guns.

Gordon MacDonald

Even amongst Christians it is possible to find envy. Not necessarily of possessions but of position, power or success. Gordon MacDonald writes of feeling threatened, when a young pastor, by the success of others. It seems that when we are united and doing the same kind of work for God, it is possible to inflict such wounds on each other that it can mean withdrawal of someone from the battle.

We can inflict and receive wounds from "friendly" guns in almost every sector of church life or Christian service, but if our friendship with God is right, then it extends in loyal and loving friendship to his people. We shall be as concerned that God's work is being well done, whoever is doing it, and hopefully be willing to help and sustain the one who is doing it.

We are all less strong and more sensitive than is apparent, and realizing this in others should help us in our understanding of one another. To be behind a gun that fires at friends, merely rebounds and leaves a resentment that holds us in thrall.

Go home to your friends and tell them what wonderful things God has done for you, and how merciful he has been.

Gospel of Mark

Jesus spoke these words to a demon-possessed man whom he had healed. He sent the demons into a herd of swine that plunged into a lake and drowned. The man then begged Jesus that he might go along with him. It was a perfectly natural request, for many travelled with Jesus, but it was a request that Jesus denied. The man was instead told to go home, but to go home with a purpose, to tell what had been done for him by God. For this man life had completely changed; it was indeed a miracle, but he obeyed.

A part of our friendship with others is that they should know about the way God deals with us. We share the things of God together, and by telling others we bring glory to God; we show the wonderful things that he does in our life. For some, friendship may mean going to those who do not understand and speaking of what he means to us. Or helping in situations where we can show the love of God. It may even mean staying in a situation when we would rather be elsewhere, in order that others may know about God.

When you please the Lord you can make your enemies your friends.

Proverbs

No one cares to have enemies, and the Christian least of all. It gives a feeling of failure, and we regret giving someone cause to dislike us because of something that we may have done. Circumstances do sometimes lead to another person disliking us intensely, but we should not be content with the situation. The New International Version of the Bible gives this verse as: "When a man's ways are pleasing to the Lord, he makes even his enemies live at peace with him." What is it that can alter a situation like this?

Firstly, we must be pleasing God. The way in which we live our life has to please him. If we always try to show kindness in our dealings with others, seeking to understand them and not to give in to the temptation of retaliating to anything that may be done to us, we shall have peace.

Secondly, it must be brought to God in prayer. The whole situation must be covered in prayer. It has been suggested that the reading each day of the thirteenth chapter of Corinthians, plus prayer, will bring about a change. The change will be in us too, as we allow the Holy Spirit to do the work.

All but the best friends flinched away.

Margaret Spufford

14

Life sometimes makes demands on us which we have to resolve as we think best for all those involved in the situation. Even as a Christian among Christians this is not always understood. It can lead to the kind of situation that Margaret Spufford found. She and her husband wanted to make home life as normal as possible for the family when their daughter was found to have a chronic illness. Faced with the fact that she would die without constant nursing attention, and in any case had a limited life span, they had to adopt a lifestyle that obviously deterred friendship.

To have friends leave because you are doing what you believe is right is incredibly hurtful, especially in a situation which is already making great demands. Friends are meant to be there in those moments when help is most needed. Ideally, they should be supportive, whatever they feel about the situation. The quotation underlines that there are those who take friendship seriously, they are "best" friends trying to show and give God's love.

Thou hast restored me again to the friendship of God.

Thomas Traherne

Mediators are those who bring reconciliation between two parties. What joy we can find when we are able to help in this task of bringing new thinking and peace where there has previously been distrust and animosity. How wonderful, too, is the joy of those who have been reconciled, when they have restored friendship.

The great Mediator is Jesus Christ, who through his life and death reconciles us to God. Thomas Traherne is aware of the greatness of his debt to his Lord, that through him "heaven and earth are infinitely more valuable than they were before". He sees that this brings an enjoyment of the world and a "hope of eternal glory". Life — and death — is completely different for us (or should be), once we have accepted the reconciliation process and the work of the Mediator.

Above all, we are restored to friendship with God, which is an openness of heart between two people. This is the work which the Mediator has done. The barriers have gone, brought down by the reconciliatory work of the Cross which Jesus accomplished. As a result, life becomes more sweet, our goals become different and we go forward with the hope of eternal life.

A friend of Jesus dares all and never says such and such is too hard.

Ruth Burrows

Friendship with Jesus is the greatest friendship of all. We have the tremendous privilege of being brought into this relationship with God, but all friendship has its responsibilities and commitment. Commitment to Jesus means a high level of trust; it means that we are aware of being able to do all the things that he demands, in his strength. It is a stepping out in faith when situations develop, when the way begins to get hard.

Life is made up of daily problems, large or small. None of us is immune from the pain and disappointments that come into every life. The difference is in the way in which we tackle our problems and accept the set-backs. Walking with God means believing that with him it is possible to work through everything.

We remember that life is not all sorrow and pain. Each day also contains joys and happiness. These, too, are a part of our life with him and to be accepted with thanksgiving and shared with others. We do God's will but we also accept God's will. Trusting in him and his friendship means believing that, through all, he will make us to be more like him.

There are false friends who are there to laugh when we laugh, but not to weep when we weep.

Jean Vanier

It is sometimes difficult to discern who is a real friend until there is trouble. Everyone is willing to laugh, and whilst there is always laughter then friends will be around. When there are difficulties, trouble, illness or death, then some of those who call themselves friends suddenly disappear.

Unfortunately, Christians often find that when most needed some of their friends are unable to enter into a situation that embarrasses them. They cannot weep with those who weep. Jesus wept when he heard of the death of his friend Lazarus, and he understood the grief of Mary and Martha when he went to them. It seems inconceivable to us that he cannot feel the pain that we have; yet we can refuse to show that we share the pain of our friends.

The commitment to our friends is to be faithful to our friendship with them; to be with them when they are in need; to show them the love and tenderness they may be wanting; to listen and sometimes just to do the practical things that are needed to be done. The Holy Spirit wants to use us in helping those in distress, just as he uses others to give to us.

In and through God we can be faithful to each other: in friendship, marriage and community.

Henri Nouwen

In our world most people walk a path of fear and lack of confidence. There is a lack of freedom to express oneself fully. It is these things that build up a barrier so that we find it difficult to give ourselves to others in, as Nouwen suggests, friendship, marriage or community. In each of these the necessity is to forge a relationship with one or more other people. If we are totally absorbed with ourselves and our inhibitions then we cannot give ourselves to others.

It is when we have established a relationship with God, undergirded by prayer, that we find he enables us to release self into his care. As we find a new confidence in the one who is perfect in his love we are able to reach a new freedom which brings a fresh awareness of what friendship can be. The more our life is knit with his, the easier it is to be faithful in our relationships.

"Freedom is what we have — Christ has set us free", says the writer to the Galatians. It is a complete freedom that we have in Christ, and in which we should make every effort to walk.

Jesus loves you like a friend. He holds out his hand to you.
Give him yours.

Basilea Schlink

A parent continually insists on a young child holding their hand, for they know that in this way the child is kept safe, and protected. Brother Ramon, in writing of this situation with his father says, "Of course I was to hold tightly to him, but I also knew that whether I held on or not, he would hold me."

To take the hand of God is not only a sign of accepting his friendship but means also that he will hold us and give to us his strength and protection. It means that we stay close and walk in step with him. Accepting his friendship means that we give him our trust and believe that he will always do what is best for us. Just as the young child has perfect confidence in the person who is holding his hand, so can we have the same confidence in the One of whom the Psalmist says, "He is my refuge and my fortress, my God, in whom I trust".

The love of Jesus is always seeking out those who need him, and with whom he wants to share his friendship. Our response is to put our hand in his.

He [God] wants me as his friend and desires to be my friend and has given his Son to die for me in order to realize this purpose.

J.I. Packer

To want to be friends with someone means that we are willing to take the time to get to know them — in a sense we explore them — their minds, their tastes, their attitudes and the way they go about things. God reveals himself to us as we take the time to know him, and the more we want to know him so he shows us how we can come to know him better. A casual relationship with God is of no real satisfaction to us, neither does it bring joy to him. As he has chosen us for friendship, so does he long for a true and deep relationship with us.

Packer suggests that friendship with God is also emotional, that being involved with God means desiring to please him and keep his laws. It means being glad when he is honoured and sad when he is made of no account. It must also mean being concerned about his affairs in the world, and seeking to advance them by prayer and witness. It also means listening to God, for only as we learn to hear what he says can we know what he wants of us.

Friends and partners are wise to apologize and forgive one another at once.

Mark Gibbard SSJE

It is inevitable that at times a rift comes into our friendships. We cannot always agree with a friend, and we may express our opinion too strongly, which leads to a disagreement, or some other misunderstanding may occur. To allow it to drift merely causes more coldness and trouble. It is indeed a good thing to resolve the problem immediately and be quickly reconciled.

If this is something that we want to do with our friends because we dislike having a rift between us, how much more should we desire always to be right with God. If God is our friend then surely we do not want to experience those same cold periods with him. We sometimes experience impatience with God, believing that he should be doing certain things for us. Or we can do things that we know are not right, and we fail and grieve him. Whatever it is, we should not let anything come between us. As with all matters that have to be put right, the longer we leave it the longer it takes.

"We don't want", says Gibbard, "small faults to build up into a wedge either between us and those we love or between us and God."

The greatest love that man can have is to give his life for his friends.

Gospel of John (Barclay translation)

Tucked among some of the most wonderful words that Jesus spoke to his disciples, is this sentence. Because it is so true, the disciples may not have understood at the time its greater meaning, but as we read it today we know that it refers to the death of Jesus.

When John the Baptist saw Jesus coming towards him he said, "Look, the Lamb of God, who takes away the sin of the world!" In the Old Testament the sacrifice of an animal was given to God, in the New, Jesus himself became the sacrifice and it was this that the Baptist recognized as he saw Jesus. Friends do give their life for a friend when they see the need, and God foresaw the need and sent Jesus to die for his friends. To die for another denotes a great love, and other words of Jesus — "God so loved the world that he gave his one and only son . . ." — reveal the love that God has for us.

Sin demands a sacrifice, and although sin is our disobedience to God, he provided the sacrifice and opened up the way back to himself. A friend gave his life for us.

In the world it is necessary to be bound together in friendship, to stimulate each other in doing good.

Francis de Sales

Christians are meant to help each other as they travel the same path; to help one another to the spiritual best. Our world is one of pressures, where between work, church and home, we put in long hours. There are demands on time and money. The very circumstances of our lives are demanding as we need to make decisions, deciding what is the right thing to do in so many situations. God is our helper, but in this world we also need friends who will support us and keep us "on target" — friends who want to care.

So it is that we should respond to friendship when it is offered, answering the unexpected letters that come and are written in kindness, and initiating the phone call instead of always waiting for someone to ring. To be too independent borders on the sin of pride, and as individuals and families we need the stimulus of friends. It is our friends who broaden our thoughts about the world in which we live; who often underline our own thinking on different topics; who lead us into greater understanding of spiritual truths; and who frequently keep our feet on the right way with practical advice.

Nothing in heaven or earth or hell can separate us from the love of God; we should see to it that nothing on earth shall separate us from God's friendship.

A.W. Tozer

Tozer appears to be suggesting here that whilst God's love for us is eternal, the type of friendship that we have with God is to a certain extent in our own hands. "Nothing", he says, "is important enough to be allowed to stand in the way of our relation to God."

Our friendship with God is the ongoing relationship that means growth in spirituality. Christianity is not only accumulating knowledge about our faith, but becoming more like God himself. This is the core of what friendship with God is about, but because friendship needs time and effort we have to make sure that we spend the time necessary to draw ever closer to God. It has to be a priority in our life; mind and will needs to be set to put God first.

Wanting to be holy as God is holy also means that we want quickly to put right anything that has gone wrong between us. Sin separates us from God, and allowing it to stay in our life would certainly cause a separation. The remembrance that God wants us as a friend should be enough for us to crave his friendship and to guard it at all cost.

Friendship is based on the staying power of love.

Andrea Midgett

Friendship is demanding, and if we refuse to accept its demands we lose a great part of what life is about. For a variety of reasons we need each other, and our life is enriched by our friendships. We realize that in accepting the rewards that come from knowing our friends, we in turn must be available to them. There has to be an acceptance of those things that we like least in them, remembering that we ourselves must certainly have a few quirks.

It takes an effort of time as well; keeping in touch makes a demand, and if we are not willing to make that effort we may be denying someone the continuance of our friendship. The staying power in friendship comes from our own walk with the Lord. The more that we draw from him, the more we have to give to others. The more we understand his mind, the more we discern the needs of our friends and can be the support that is sometimes needed. We pray for our friends and in our love stand by them in good and bad times. We show interest in all that concerns them, and are willing to be needed.

Each day Lord,
Help me to be open and receptive
To those who need my friendship.

Frank Topping

If we are honest with ourselves, there are times when we run away from the possibility of friendship with a particular person. We may sense that they would like to get to know us, but we may feel that the effort involved is just too much. Getting to know others, though, is surely a part of our life of following Christ. Sometimes involvement with another is the opportunity of showing God's love. We cannot think of Jesus ever refusing to give to someone in need. Not only was he quick to sense a need that was real, but we can imagine the interest and concern that accompanied his desire to help.

Each day we can be alert to the kind of friendship that is needed by someone who is perhaps shy or lonely, or even is just needing to have someone acknowledge that they are there. Friendship can be on many levels, and we should be willing for each as they appear. Not every friendship will be a deep one, but every friendship can be worthwhile and give a satisfaction. Being open and allowing others to see us as we are is the beginning of reaching out to them.

Moses, the friend of Yahweh.

William Johnston

We read in Exodus that "The Lord would speak to Moses face to face, as a man speaks with his friend". Moses was called by God to lead the Israelites out of Egypt. In the process of seeking to obey, Moses came to know God. He met God and God spoke to him, "face to face", relaying through him what he wanted the people to know. It is not possible to see the face of God, but Moses was able to come close to him and to hear his voice.

One day Moses asked to see God's glory, and God said, "I will put you in a cleft of the rock and cover you with my hand until I have passed by. Then I will remove my hand and you will see my back; but my face must not be seen". We read also that when he spoke with the Lord, "his face was radiant".

When Moses was disobedient over the striking of the rock, the Lord told him that he would not go into the Promised Land. He only viewed it and it was there he died, and where God buried Moses, his friend, secretly.

We cannot compare one love or friendship with another, because each is so distinct and unusual that it stands alone on its own merits.

Chester P. Michael and Marie C. Norrisey

A little thought about the friends that we have may astonish us by the different type of people that they are, and also, by the different type of person we become in their company. With some we laugh more; with others we give; from some we receive. We pray with some; we discuss with others; we share different pursuits with different people. This does not make one friend necessarily any more important than another; in fact, what we draw from one enables us to contribute something that enriches another friendship.

It is pleasing to remember that God in his friendships with his people must also find something similar. It does not seem impossible that he enjoys the sunny nature, just as he understands the more meditative one, that he is to our personalities as we are to the personalities of our friends. We are all different, and this is perhaps why we should never resent the way in which God deals with us, or compare the circumstances that he has given us to those of others. Our friendship with God is unique; we each bring something that is essentially of us to it; each is a special relationship.

Christianity is — quite simply — a matter of friendship with
Jesus Christ.

Florence Allshorn

For some, friendship with Christ may seem an unfamiliar thought. Their approach to God is that of a reverence that does not admit of anything bordering on the familiar. Yet if we examine the gospels we see that Jesus had friends. He was received in homes; there were those who were concerned for him and helped him. He, in turn, drew around him a special band to whom he opened his heart. He told them all about himself, why he had come, who his Father was, and what the relationship between them was like. He told them about his home and all the things that he wanted for his friends.

He knew each one; knew all about them and was not dismayed when they were unable to be perfect people; he loved them. He told them that when he had to leave them, his Father would send the Holy Spirit in his place. So it is that we have within us the Spirit of God, and the more we acknowledge his presence the more we come to know him. He is our unseen, inner companion, our true friend, and following Christ means having this wonderful friendship with him.

But friendship, like forgiveness, must be total.

Catherine de Hueck Doherty

Once we are able to forgive someone, then the way is open for friendship, and as forgiveness means putting away completely whatever was the cause of resentment, so friendship should be entered into wholeheartedly. Once the barrier has been broken down, then there is nothing to stop the sharing which comes with friendship. The important thing is that the forgiveness must be total. Even though we may not actually forget what has been done to us, forgiveness means that all hurt has gone, and the person is treated as if nothing had happened.

If for some reason we do not forgive in the right sense of that word, then total friendship is impossible, for we shall also be unable to trust, and without trust we shall not be free to care.

Once the whole situation of our forgiveness has been gone through with God, then we can enter into a friendship with him. Whilst always realizing that it was the need for forgiveness that first raised the barrier between us, when this is down, knowledge and trust enable a total friendship. We are freed to share life with him but, as with our human friendships, any reservations mean that the relationship is not total.

The more perfect our friendship with God becomes the simpler will our lives be.

A.W. Tozer

Tozer writes, "Unquestionably the highest privilege granted to man on earth is to be admitted into the circle of the friends of God". We shall always have God's love, but friendship with God should be the natural outcome of the moment when we understand that we belong to him. As with most friendships, it takes a certain amount of time before a real relationship is achieved. There is a period when there is the need to find out about each other's ways and thinking.

It is the same with friendship with God. He, being perfect, does not have to learn about us, nor about the ways of friendship. We, however, need to get to know him; learn that we can trust him; spend time with him until we desire to be like him. Prayer, the study of the Scriptures, and a determination to serve him, will mean the growth of friendship with God. The time will come when we shall only want to please him, and as in a good friendship where there is not always need for words, we shall feel comfortable just being quiet in his presence.

This is what Tozer means; as friendship grows so there is less need for formalities. Knowledge and trust take over.

This is princely friendship from our courteous Lord that he still sustains us secretly even while we are in sin.

Julian of Norwich

Julian is reminding us of a wonderful truth: that once we have given ourselves to God our sin does not separate us from him. How often have we experienced times when we feel that because we have failed him in some way, it must mean that he wants nothing more to do with us?

In fact what he actually does is to seek to make us understand that he still loves us; that failures can be put right; and that continually he is working in our lives in order that we should be like him.

In his friendship there is a gentleness, an understanding. He knows about our failures, the times when we fall far short of the best that he wants for us. He knows that they tend to make us hide ourselves away from him because we are ashamed. He just quietly waits and works for that moment when we turn back to find him. In the times when we are unconscious of having fallen into sin, then God gently makes us aware, pouring out his grace and mercy.

This is our God, "our courteous Lord", who does not turn in anger against us but seeks only our growth.

Jesus knew what it meant to be deserted and betrayed, and denied by his family and friends.

Gonville ffrench-Beytagh

Family, we feel, may not always understand us, but when we think of our friends we anticipate a degree of knowledge and same-thinking that means we shall always be understood by them. Unfortunately, this may not be the case. There may be paths along which they can no longer walk with us. They may feel that circumstances change loyalty. We have probably all felt rejected at some time, and known the loneliness that this can bring. To be in a situation of betrayal means wounding and pain.

Friendship certainly brings happiness, but it sometimes brings sorrow. It needs an inner strength to bear up and go on when we feel deserted. Jesus rejoiced in his friendships, but how badly he must have felt when most of his friends were unable to stand by him, even though he understood, and his feelings did not change towards them.

On the day that we may have to go through this kind of despair we can remember that he knows, because he too has been through it. He continued to love his friends, and we too will have to draw from him so that we do not harbour the hurt and resentment that can embitter us.

The moment I exclude God from my friendship then things will start to go wrong.

Michael Buckley

Belonging to God, which means that he is the primary person in our life, should mean that he is a part of everything that we touch. If he is not a part of our friendship then there is something very wrong, both with our life with God and the way in which we look upon our friends.

Friendship means adjustments; we have to be prepared for growth in others as well as in ourselves, and be willing to share both. God expects us to give to others what he reveals to us on a spiritual level. His love is given out through us and should encourage others to be drawn to him; our thinking should be for their good, and to help them to achieve the best.

If we try to maintain friendship in and through our own humanity, things will indeed go wrong. As Christians, the love that we have for God and for our friend is intertwined. The love for our friend grows because of knowing God's love and realizing what we both mean to him, and as love grows so the nearer do we come to understanding the life God means his children to live.

Friendship with the world is hatred towards God.

Letter of James

We live in the world and therefore have to be a part of it, but the Bible continually warns us against desiring the things of the world rather than concentrating on the things of God. The Scriptures liken the relationship between God and his people to that of marriage. The Church is the bride of Christ, and when James writes, "You adulteress people, don't you know that friendship with the world is hatred towards God?" he is emphasizing this relationship.

It is possible for our hearts to be wooed away by the things of the world; for our minds to feed on those things that do not help us spiritually and can eventually become more important to us than pleasing God. It is this which is likened to adultery — the unfaithfulness of one partner.

When once we allow our thinking to be the same as that of the world around us, then our allegiance has been transferred. The word "hatred" is a strong one, but the more we desire a self-pleasing life, the more there grows the feeling of friendship for the world which leads to its opposite, a lessening of the desire to love and serve God.

It is easy to cultivate the friendship of the person who can do things for us, and whose influence can be useful to us.

William Barclay

The person who sets out to find friends for any selfish reason will not find friendship. Barclay is suggesting that it is an easy thing to set out to be friendly towards those who can be of help to us. What we are actually doing is putting on an act, pretending, for the worst of motives. We may even find that we make a habit of cultivating those who can be useful to us or are acclaimed in our society.

The opposite side of the coin is that we spurn those who have nothing to give for our advancement. It is easy to look on the circumstances and outward appearance of someone and then turn aside. This was never the way of Jesus. He seemed so often to seek out those who were the least in society, and his feeling for them was always apparent. The Pharisees and the teachers of the law saw him doing what they would not do — eating with tax collectors and sinners — mixing with the lowest.

Friendship means being a helper when help is needed. Giving, not for the thought of a return but for the sheer delight of being in the position that God wants of us.

He called them friends who have been especially chosen.

Bryan Gilbert

It might be said that we do not exactly choose our friends. Friendships seem more to grow out of being acquainted, although the "let's be best friends" of childhood does suggest a spontaneity and a deliberate choosing. To be chosen in such a way makes us feel very good.

Part of the wonder of our relationship with God is that we have been chosen. As individuals we have been singled out, we are known. In the Gospel of John, Jesus, speaking to his disciples, says two important things: "I have called you friends . . ." and "You did not choose me, but I chose you . . ." We are not servants who merely do as they are told to do, but friends who have the confidence of the Master.

Then we see that we have been chosen for friendship, but more than that, chosen to "bear fruit". Chosen, so that out of the friendship we will be able to show others the One who is our Friend, and the person that he is, by the way in which we act and live out our life. We have been chosen for a task which in joy we should seek to accomplish, remembering his joy in us.

He helps, he strengthens, he never fails, he is the true Friend.

Teresa of Avila

It is when looking at Jesus that we see the true meaning of friendship, and our experience of walking with him reveals the essential ingredients of this loving relationship. If, therefore, we desire to be a friend to others we need only draw from him. As he is to us so we may be to another.

He is the one who is always wanting to help us as we travel through each day. He understands the way we feel and does not condemn, rather does he seek to pour in his strength in order that we may have the courage that we may be needing. He is always available to us and we may be sure that we will not be let down by him. God gives us much and we need to be aware of the great truths that make up his gift of salvation, but if we want to make things simple for everyday living we can remember that we have the gift of his friendship.

Day by day we may walk in that friendship with him, and as Teresa of Avila says, "With so good a Friend and Captain, himself the first to suffer, everything can be borne".

We accept His friends as our friends.

A.W. Tozer

The saddest thing that one can hear is of Christians who are at loggerheads with each other. There is the true story of two ministers, one a black man, the other white, who continually vilified each other, and it was not until their bishop spoke separately to them when on retreat, that matters changed. He suggested that they had not allowed Jesus to enter into this part of their lives. The men were broken down, and when later they met in a passage they fell into each other's arms.

"To accept Christ is to know the meaning of the words 'as he is, so are we in this world' ", writes Tozer. Jesus was never disparaging about his followers, and if we are following him, we are to be like him in every way. We are to accept his friends as our friends and act towards them in the way that pleases him. This may not be easy, and perhaps this has to be acknowledged. It is acknowledging the truth that paves the way for restoration and healing. It is allowing Jesus to break down our resentments and prejudices, replacing them with peace and love, that enables Christians to walk together as friends.

You make more friends by becoming interested in other people than by trying to interest other people in yourself.

Dale Carnegie

No one could say that Jesus was not interested in other people. He continually showed this by his thought and care for those around him. He entered into their feelings and the circumstances of their situation, and many were drawn to him and gave him their help and friendship in return.

We see something of this when we meet someone for the first time. Their interest in us causes us to respond, but only if there is a give and take of interest in each other is there the possibility of friendship developing. Friendship is not one way. Where anyone is only concerned with him- or herself and the acquiring of a group around them, then this is not friendship.

Perhaps we can say that we cannot go out to make friends for purely selfish reasons, for when this is attempted then the basis for friendship fades away. The Christian life teaches us to forget selfish interests, and it is from this premise that we can reach out to others with the possibility of growing and mutual concern that leads to friendship. It is not, however, the possibility of friendship that should press us, but a love for others.

This friend of mine . . . was so anchored in God and filled with love for me that, intuitively, she knew when to write, what to say and how to pray.

Joyce Huggett

Joyce Huggett was writing about a friend who had died, and she tells how this friend had loved and prayed for her. "It was as though, through her prayer, she touched God with one hand and through the depth of her care touched me with the other."

There will always be a time when a friend needs more from us than they are able, at that time, to return. It may mean having to spend extra time with God in order to have the right words to speak. There may have to be a sitting down and just listening to words coming from a wounded heart; of having eyes to see where practical help is needed, for being practical can be as needful as every other kind of help.

To help a friend we shall need to approach God to fill us with his love for the needs of this person. We shall have to be sensitive to the Holy Spirit within us, in order to appreciate what this friend is wanting, not just from us, but perhaps from God himself. We may need to be a go-between, touching God and our friend.

Jonathan, the crown prince, recognized in David a kindred spirit, and struck up a deep friendship with him.

Joyce Baldwin

The friendship between Jonathan, the son of Saul, and David, is famous. We read that "Jonathan made a covenant with David because he loved him as himself". At that time Jonathan took off his robe, his tunic, his sword, his bow and his belt, and gave them to David. This action of giving his royal insignia appears to be a giving up, even of his right to the throne, in favour of David.

Jonathan remained true to the friendship even in the face of his father's growing animosity towards David; the Bible tells us again that Jonathan loved David as himself. When Jonathan is killed, with his brothers, and Saul himself commits suicide, David laments, but it is for Jonathan that he feels pain. His friend who has loved him, has been true to him, has renounced his own rights for him.

This is a picture of friendship, with its seeming discernment on the part of Jonathan of what was in store for David, but with no apparent jealousy. Friendship, then, is more than an easy give and take. It is having the good of the other very much in our thoughts and as a point to our actions.

There is a friend who sticks closer than a brother.

Proverbs

Blood, we say, is thicker than water, meaning that we can expect family to be more of a help in a crisis than any friend. Here we have the thought that there are friends who do more for us than even a close relative. There may of course be many reasons for this: opportunity; they have the help we need; they may be more on our wavelength because of belief. It may be that they have a deeper interest in our welfare. To those who serve us in such a way we need to accept their friendship in love, and with a reciprocation of their care.

Such a friend reminds us of the one who is the perfect friend. The more we come to know Jesus and how he cares for us, the more we are able to emulate him in our friendships. The closer we are to him, the closer we find that we draw to others. As we take time to listen to Jesus so is our thinking more like his. As we pray, our concern and love grows for those for whom we are praying. As he never lets us down, so should we stand by our friends.

Then he brought together the twelve he had called to become his friends.

Jean Vanier

74

Jesus called together men and women to follow him, and to enter into a special relationship with himself. He called twelve men who became an inner circle, but there were many more who followed him and were his disciples. The twelve he sought to teach and to prepare for the special task of working with him, and for the day when he would be taken from them. They were his friends and he knew them intimately, loved them.

The twelve were a very mixed bunch. Not only did they come from varied backgrounds but their temperaments were also very different: dear, volatile Peter, calm, loving John, doubting Thomas, muddled, unfaithful Judas. They bickered amongst themselves, they misunderstood what Jesus was telling them, they hoped for glory, nearly all fled when Jesus appeared to be disgraced.

In spite of this and more, Jesus called them his friends. He knew everything about them. At the end when they were together to share a last meal, he wrapped a towel round his waist and began to wash and dry the feet of his disciples and, "having loved his own who were in the world, he now showed them the full extent of his love".

The fact that God has a relationship of friendship with people is a sign of his unchanging faithfulness.

Martin Manser

God has committed himself to his people and it is this which is the basis of the relationship, a relationship of love and friendship, and because of it we can be sure that his promise of being our God continues through all our life. He is a faithful God, and daily we learn to trust him.

A friendship is, however, a growing thing as each gets to know the other. Our friendship with God should be continually growing and changing as we understand more of his working in our lives. In a sense we test the faithfulness of God as day by day we turn to him and rely on him, and as we find that he is faithful so does the friendship deepen. It deepens with each new understanding that we have of his way with us.

He provides for us, and we see his faithfulness in material and spiritual ways. He does not only make sure that we have sufficient for our daily needs, but beginning "a good work in you will continue it until it is completed on the day when Jesus Christ comes". He saves us and continues our salvation through to the end.

Without Jesus, your friends . . . are going to hell.

Joseph C. Aldrich

Many of us are not what we ourselves would call evangelists. We may even feel embarrassed if we have to talk to others about the things that we believe. It becomes different when we start thinking that unless our friends know about Jesus and opt for him they will not be allowed into heaven. Heaven is a place of light, love and purity. Hell is the exact opposite, a place that is cut off from God and all that is good.

A part of friendship is wanting the best for our friends, and if we know something about the love of God we shall want them to know about it also. So our life must be such that through all the chores of daily living we show something of the character of God. We have to watch and be ready for that moment when we can actually speak words that not only bring help and comfort but can also point to God.

Friendship is about loving; being a Christian is about following Christ and revealing his love to others. Together they should cause us to want to know that our friends will understand the pathway to peace and heaven.

The mark of perfect friendship is not that help will be given when the pinch comes (of course it will) but that, having been given, it makes no difference at all.

C.S. Lewis

C.S. Lewis would seem to be writing here about the friendship between men, which is probably quite different to that between women. Men appear to be concerned with talking around ideas and subjects; being with one another. More personal things, such as family and background, do not seem to be so important. However, friendship, whether between men or women, does not impose a sort of blackmail when help is given.

We read in the Bible of a party of men who came to Jesus, four of them carrying a paralytic. How interesting it would be to have some more information. We only know that a whole group of people were concerned about him. They all believed that Jesus could help their friend — they were determined to get him to Jesus, and they went to a great deal of trouble. Being unable to reach Jesus they went up to the roof and made an opening to let the man down.

We can imagine the joy of the whole group when the paralytic was healed and able to walk. We read that Jesus saw *their* faith, and forgave the man his sins. The group were one in thinking and in care for their friend.

If we wish to know what the real God, who longs for our friendship, is like, let us look . . . at Jesus.

Mark Gibbard SSJE

God reveals himself in Jesus. We may have all kinds of preconceived ideas about God, but to know him as he really is we must look at Jesus. Jesus, who found happiness with his friends, turning the water into wine; and sensitive to the hungry crowd by giving them food. He was aware of the needs of people and took time with them. We remember the woman of Samaria; the woman taken in adultery; the woman ill for twelve years. Jesus knew that blind Bartimaeus wanted him to help; he touched the lepers; he sorrowed with Mary and Martha when Lazarus died. Always he was accessible, concerned, loving.

Jesus said, "I and the Father are one". As we see Jesus we see the God who loves us and longs for our friendship. Does this seem to be something too wonderful to be true? Does God really want that kind of relationship? If our image of God is of someone severe and judgemental it needs to be revised in the light of the life of Jesus and what he said. God's tremendous love, care and desire for each one of us is shown by that life — and death.

Not only can friendship be the answer to loneliness, it can also provide the basis for creating a place where we can help each other to flourish and grow.

Grace Sheppard

For some, making friends is not an easy matter. There may have been problems in the past, where perhaps friendships have been betrayed and it then becomes difficult to trust again. We need friends, however; to know that someone cares, that there is at least one person who will receive us when we are needing solace. Perhaps it is that we have to accept the betrayals and continue to give out in friendship, not seeking it so much for ourselves but that we may give to others, for it is in giving that we receive.

Grace Sheppard writes of "creating a place". This must mean that we have to work at making a place where the friendship will flourish and grow.

We need each other. It is as we communicate together on all levels that we help each other to grow. We learn to trust one another, and out of this trust comes the ability to confide. Where two are seeking to follow God so the Holy Spirit is able to enter into the friendship and use it to help both to "flourish", for friend will seek the best for friend, and this means the desire to see spiritual advancement in each other.

On the dark days, we need the refuge of friendship.

Jean Vanier

"The Holy Spirit uses small things to comfort and strengthen us", writes Jean Vanier. How true it is that when we are feeling low, a letter or a phone call can lift our spirits. The very thought that someone has remembered us and taken the trouble to get in touch can be very uplifting. That the Holy Spirit reaches out through others just to give that moment of encouragement is heart warming.

Whilst we are happy to receive in such a manner we need to remember that we also can be used to give the same help. We must not be so wrapped up in our own family, our own doings, that we forget the needs of our friends. There are promises to remember, perhaps a prayer to be said, but essentially there is the basic showing of friendship — a remembering that they are there, and doing something to show that they are valued. For them, a letter could mean the sun coming down through a dark cloud.

Friendship is a call to faithfulness. Entering into friendship with someone means becoming committed to them and to their needs, as they are to us. It means being available.

Jesus calls his friends to community, where they live and share together.

Jean Vanier

Community is very much on the heart of Jean Vanier, who has founded two, and it is something which we hear more of in these days. Extended families are also more commonplace, but many of us would say that this is not a life that appeals, and would go to the other extreme of withdrawal.

What we should all have, perhaps, is a "community heart". A heart that wants to share. The giving to each other that shows the true unity of those who belong to the family of God. Not only, and specifically, the signing of a cheque but allowing the friends of Jesus, who must also be our friends, to enter into our life and to be willing to enter into theirs.

Sharing does mean the sharing of material goods but it also means the sharing of sorrows, of problems as well as joys, and spiritual lessons. It can mean sharing our fears, of learning to be less independent. The church family should be the place of community, where we share in the communal life of seeking to serve God and one another. It is the place of growth as we give and take from each other.

Love and friendship do not grow if we are not prepared to sacrifice a great deal for their sake.

Metropolitan Anthony

Friendship is nothing without love, and neither can grow unless they are nurtured. The person without friends is the person who is unable to reach out to others, who begrudges the time it takes to get to know someone and to enter into their feelings. There is no true friendship if only one person is doing the giving.

Friendship with God means having an understanding of how he feels about us, and wanting to give in return. We need to know what he wants of us to ensure the growth of the relationship. We have to try to please him, to do our part in the friendship. It is an opening up of ourselves to his love, being prepared to take the time to read what he says in the Scriptures, to pray and to be quiet with him.

Metropolitan Anthony suggests that we may even have to put aside many things in order to give God the first place, and it is true that we have to be willing to push aside things, and even people, in order that our life with God is given the opportunity to grow.

God is the friend of man.

Michael Ramsey

To think of God as a friend gives a great feeling of awe. We can readily understand the fact of God loving us, but friendship seems to be so much more intimate. It suggests giving and taking, knowledge, a familiarity, all of which appears alien in our thinking of an Almighty God. To be loved by such a person is truly wonderful, but to be wanted as a friend, for God to act as a friend, is almost beyond understanding.

It is perhaps in our human friendships that we see something of the self-giving that is in the nature of God, and begin to understand what fellowship with him is meant to be. We are inclined to put ourselves out for our friends, to be willing to give them time and help. We seek to understand their feelings, to comfort, to laugh with them, to enjoy them, to be honest with them.

God is our friend because he is for us. He is the perfect friend, the One who is always showing us what friendship is about. The whole meaning behind his giving of himself at Easter was that we could be together. *There* he showed himself as a friend.

A friend loves at all times.

Proverbs

The biggest test of love and friendship comes when a friend has brought some sort of trouble on her- or himself. It is so easy to go along with others and refuse to associate further with the one who was a friend. It is at times such as these that we have to consider seriously what we mean by friendship.

To love a friend at all times means standing with them in all kinds of situations. It means thinking of their needs, rather than wondering how what they are, or what they are doing, is going to react on us. It means putting ourselves out to help in whatever way is possible; to be available.

We might think of Jesus's friends, most of whom ran away when he was in need of their support. There was Judas, who was continually with Jesus yet in the end betrayed him; and Peter, who was so frightened at being associated with Jesus when all were against him. We see how for the disciples the whole situation was beyond their understanding, and so they reacted accordingly. Jesus did not change, his love for them continued through all.

There comes a moment . . . when an acquaintance becomes a friend.

Basil Hume OSB

96

We all have acquaintances, people whom we meet and who fit into the outer circle of our life. It is from this circle that our friends come. As we get to know someone we find that we enjoy each other's company; it makes us want to meet more often; perhaps do things together. Then we find that we can confide in one another, that trust has grown up and we are friends.

Something like this happens in our relationship with God. We may have meetings on a regular weekly basis when we attend church, but fail to bring him into our life. Meeting each Sunday seems to be sufficient, until gradually we find that we are beginning to think about God during the week.

Slowly something builds up between us, until as Basil Hume writes, "There comes a moment". A moment when we realize that we are learning to trust this person, that it is possible to confide in him, that the relationship has become important. God has become a friend, with all that this means in terms of true friendship. He is no longer just a Sunday acquaintance but a friend for every day in the week.

Friendship is mutual love, and unless it is mutual it is not friendship.

Francis de Sales

It is possible to love without having love returned. God himself loves all his creatures, but in so many cases that love is not returned. Therefore there can be no friendship. It is when love is reciprocated, when there is a give and take on all levels, that the relationship becomes friendship.

The marriage partnership should not only be one of love but one of friendship. It is not possible to have friendship without mutual liking, love and the spending of time together; therefore marriage provides the ground for the outworking of a friendship between two persons.

However, we all have friends. They come on different levels depending on the extent of what we have to give to one another; but those which deepen and are lasting are those where there is openness and frankness, where there is an understanding of, and a willingness for, the demands of friendship. It depends on being able to communicate with each other and knowing that there is a mutual affection.

Friendships are valuable, we need those who can take us as we are, respond to us, laugh with us and are willing to be helpers in times of need.

This is the comfort of friends, that though they may be said to die, yet their friendship and society are, in the best sense, ever present, because immortal.

William Penn

friendship carries with it the same interests: the ability to give and take in discussion and argument; the brushing over of weaknesses; a concern that puts itself first. True friendship covers a deep understanding of each other, and a desire to give in help and support. To love our friends in Christ means that the friendship continues even after death, for one day we shall find each other again.

How often are friends parted by circumstances, great distances perhaps, and yet the friendship continues. They can meet again as if time has never parted them. The top and bottom of each others' nature and character is known. How then shall it be when death parts them? The parting will only be for a time, and the realization of this can comfort and even make it seem as if the friendship is still continuing, which in a way it is.

We take something of our friends with us when we meet others. "In each of my friends there is something that only some other friend can fully bring out", writes C. S. Lewis. So the friendship that was ours continues after death, and can continue to enrich us and those whom we meet.

It is not enough to say that you are everybody's brother; you should be his friend too.

Rule of Life written by Father Pierre-Marie for the Jerusalem Community

Community life means that love should be given to all those within the group, and here is the further suggestion that within this community of brothers there should be an extension — that of friendship. Not only were they brothers, in other words part of the family, but they should also be friends.

This could make us reconsider some of our own relationships. Being a Christian means that we cannot look at life and situations in the same way as others. We may not react to the way that people treat us as perhaps others who are not believers do. As the brothers must not only recognize each other as a part of the community, so should we seek to be a friend to those with whom we have contact. Not only do we give to others through friendship, but we grow as we come to know them, and we learn and expand our own horizons.

There may well be times when we act as a friend to others, but this is not returned by friendship for us. This should not matter. We should be more concerned in our love, to give rather than to receive.

And the whole process is due to the action of God, who through Christ turned our enmity to himself into friendship . . .

2 Corinthians 5 (Barclay translation)

Paul, in this passage, is reminding us that when we become a Christian the "old life is gone for ever; a new life has come into being". A reconciliation takes place, for whereas we were at enmity with God that is now turned to friendship.

Enmity with God is a part of our human nature until reconciliation takes place. Many fail to realize that this is the most important step that should be made; that life is not what it should be until we find friendship with God. God always loves us, and it grieves him when we fail to take him into account as we live this life, but enmity can be turned into a glorious friendship once we desire it and see how this is possible.

God has made a way back to himself through Christ, and when we take it we enter into a new life with him, a life of friendship which alters everything, including all other friendships. No longer are we living a life that is concerned only with ourselves; instead of turning away from God, indifferent to his love, he becomes important, and life becomes truly meaningful.

Reconciliation means an ending of enmity and the making of peace and friendship between persons previously opposed.

Roy Hession

The word reconciliation contains much beauty of meaning. Anyone who has made up a quarrel or misunderstanding with another will know the peace and happiness that results. Unfortunately, we find that in our world there is often enmity; between nations; between families; between colleagues, and within all kinds of relationships. We may think it is impossible for us to love our enemy, but often when we examine the reasons we find that many of them are based on misconception.

If Jesus said that we should love our enemies then it must be possible to do so, although in trying to follow the command we may think only of sensing love. Reconciliation means far more than this. It implies an understanding of the other person and their viewpoint. It often means that there has to be an apology, and a relinquishing of all resentment so that there is a clear passage for true friendship. Something that is merely patched up does not last. Mere words do not make for peace, there has to be a heart change — a genuine desire to be reconciled, with all that this means for a continuing relationship, out of which comes peace and healing for mind and body.

God guides through the counsel of friends and godly companions.

Derek Thomas

To know the right way to take, or how to make, the correct decision is often very difficult. As Christians, we find that the whole question of guidance raises problems in itself. God has not deliberately made it difficult. There are ways in which we may become aware of how he wants us to go forward. It is perhaps because we think that it is hard to know that it becomes such a problem.

We should not expect a "writing on the wall". Rather, God expects us to think through those things that are for and against. We shall ask him in prayer that we may be guided aright, that he will give us needed wisdom. He may make something stand out in the reading of the Scriptures that gives an answer, and we shall ask the advice of our friends. Often it is our friends, who knowing us best, are able to assess the situation and give help.

This is another side of friendship as we seek wisdom in order to help a friend, but in turn we know that God will guide us through the counsel of our friends.

Blind people have overcome many obstacles . . . but it is still an unfriendly world.

Margaret Cundiff

The opposite of friendly is unfriendly, and there are many in this world who find that there is little friendship for them. Blind people find that the world has not been made for them to walk around, there are so many man-made obstacles. The disabled are usually forgotten when buildings are being erected or holidays planned; and there are many others who for one reason or another find that the world is not a friendly place.

Jesus commanded that we should love our neighbour, which surely includes befriending him. It would be impossible to make friends with everyone who has a problem, but perhaps we can somehow help to make the world a friendlier place for them. There may be people nearer to us whom we would not naturally wish to befriend, but their "blindness" of spiritual things should commend them to us, so that we could reveal to them something of God's love.

Making friends is a costly and risky business, but infinitely rewarding.

Grace Sheppard

There are some who refuse to give themselves in friendship, and this could be for a variety of reasons. One could be that having attempted to make friends nothing has come of it. This could be because not enough time was spent in assessing the rightness of a relationship, and in the end neither had anything to give to the other.

Or it could be that having started in a friendship we have been badly let down, and felt so hurt that we have not wanted to attempt such a thing again. These things do happen, but it is sad if it means that we withdraw from making close friends. Withdrawing says more about us; it suggests that we may have fears and hurt pride, and this makes us not want to get close to someone again. We can ask God to help us resolve these and to lead us to those with whom we can be friends.

To find a reward in friendship we have to match our steps with those of our friend, and be prepared to give as well as expecting to receive. We hold their confidences and make sure that each, in some way, is special to us.

With so good a Friend and Captain ever present, himself the first to suffer, everything can be borne.

Teresa of Avila

To have the Lord as a friend means that everything can be borne. His presence changes every situation and the knowledge of his love gives us strength. Margery Kempe, a fourteenth-century housewife who was also a mystic, heard God say to her: "When you go to church I go with you; when you sit down for a meal I sit with you; when you lie down to sleep I lie with you, and when you go out I go with you."

The fact that he is with us continually must alter the way in which we live our life. We shall be more conscious of the things that we do and say, but we shall also be aware of him in the difficulties of life. It means that we are not alone when ill-health, pain, or disaster strikes, but it is not enough to know that he is with us, we need to be able to talk with him, believe in his help, lean on his promises.

"To have faith is to have God", said Martin Luther. To trust him for everything means that we yield ourselves, and all that is ours, into his keeping.

Thus we find much criticism between . . . friends.

Paul Tournier

There is the story, somewhere, of four women who met and spent the entire time criticizing a friend. Later, one of the four was convicted of this and brought the matter to God for forgiveness, but it is a story that could be told over and over again concerning different groups.

It is so very easy to criticize one another, even though we in turn may be afraid of doing anything that may incur criticism. It is strange that we find it so much easier to be negative instead of positive when we speak about our friends, for there is probably much more to praise than to be criticized. If they are our friends then there must be much that we admire and like about them, and we must enjoy their company.

Jesus says, "Why do you see the speck that is in your brother's eye, but do not notice the log that is in your own eye?" Only when we have attended to the "log" that is in our own eye are we in any position to attend to the speck that we see in our friend's eye. We need to beware of being critical and judgemental towards our friends.

Praying . . . for close friends.

Frank Topping

Friendship with another is not just a question of doing things together, of mutual interests, of enjoying being together. Friendship brings certain responsibilities, for there are always times when practical help is needed or comfort and support wanted. Beneath all that makes for friendship there should be the general concern that causes us to pray.

Friendship is not just a question of the pleasure that we may get out of it: it is also being sensitive to needs that may not be expressed; of knowing when it is not speech that is needed but prayer. We shall therefore become aware of when we need especially to pray, but at the same time our friends will be on a regular prayer list, so that they will always be remembered at certain intervals.

We can pray for them, their family and their work. Knowing the kind of life that they have to lead enables definite requests to be made. It does not have to take a long time, for as we mention their names before God, he knows the details of their needs. It is in this way that we can share with our friends the ups and downs of their lives.

Abraham believed God, and it was reckoned to him as righteousness and he was called the friend of God.

Letter of James

Abraham was a man chosen by God, who obeyed the call to leave his own country and to go out into a new one. A promise was made to him that he would become great, that he would be a blessing, and that he would be the father of a great nation. At the time that Abraham was told this by God there was no way that it could be seen to be coming true — except that Abraham believed God. So at the age of seventy-five he set out.

His was a life of true adventure, and all that God had promised came to pass. This does not mean that life was easy, there were times of trial and one of great disobedience. There was friendship between God and himself; but reading the life of Abraham, many of us would find it difficult to imagine that we would have been able to do the things that he did.

It is wrong to think that people in the Bible were different. It must have been just as difficult to live a life pleasing to God then as we may find it today. It is still a matter of belief and obedience.

pleasant was a path closed by ... when chosen the call to ... have his own journey, and to govern into a new one, a ... course was made to him that he would become great that ... would be a blessing, and that he won ... to his father ... of ... ... At the time that ... she ... was told him by God on a ... was one way that a ... decision was to be made to have — except ... ... when failed to God, so at the close of his reply to be ... see ...

... was a life of quiet adventure and also ... had the ... point of great re-entry. For the ... reason that his was a mere ... there were dozens at times and most of great disorder ... re ... There ... lapped up between God and humanity ... but ... the ... of ... this strong of the whole life, ... those ... to imagine ... that we would always ... aged to be the image that we had ...

... not going to remark that people at one time were ... certain ... as most have recognize as ... their entire lives plenteously a kind ... than by getting truth ... were ... of God's nature ... but that ... obedience.

141